grief, loss and how to cope

A Self-Help Guide for Difficult Times

CHRISTOPHER SPRIGGS
AND JESS SMALLWOOD

GRIEF, LOSS AND HOW TO COPE

An Hachette UK Company
www.hachette.co.uk

Vie Books, an imprint of Summersdale Publishers Ltd
Part of Octopus Publishing Group Limited
Carmelite House
50 Victoria Embankment
LONDON
EC4Y 0DZ
UK

www.summersdale.com

Printed and bound in Poland

ISBN: 978-1-80007-396-8

Substantial discounts on bulk quantities of Summersdale books are available to corporations, professional associations and other organizations. For details contact general enquiries: telephone: +44 (0) 1243 771107 or email: enquiries@summersdale.com.

Disclaimer

Neither the author nor the publisher can be held responsible for any loss or claim arising out of the use, or misuse, of the suggestions made herein. None of the views or suggestions in this book is intended to replace medical opinion from a doctor. If you have concerns about your health, please seek professional advice.

Contents

Introduction

Welcome to this guide on grief, loss and how to cope. Grief can be unsettling and complex and is often painful because it gives rise to unfamiliar emotions and questions. Your experience will be unique to you as all loss is unique.

This guide focuses on grief and loss in all the ways it is experienced, not just from bereavement but also the loss of health, work or sense of identity.

Use this guide however you choose. Dip in and out, or flick through until a quote, tip or statement resonates with you. Highlight the parts that help, or read one page a day. There are also contact details of carefully selected organizations provided in the Resources section at the end of this book.

It takes courage to pick up a book like this, but embracing the reality of grief brings growth. Whatever your circumstances, hopefully you will find words of comfort, strength and practical support within these pages.

What is grief?

The proof of love

Grief is not an experience anyone enjoys, yet all of us will encounter it at some point during our lifetime. Grief is not a sign there is anything wrong with you, but that something significant has happened to you. It is a powerful proof of love and attachment to someone or something that holds meaning for you. Grief can be so strong, even overwhelming at times. This guide explains ways to cope, and also, in time, how to grow through the process. This might seem impossible right now and that's okay.

What is grief?

Grief is defined as "mental or emotional suffering or distress caused by loss or regret". It is an unsettling process which will prove beyond your control. Grief is not a personality disorder or a mental illness, and nor is it the same as clinical depression.

Grief may be caused by:

- A bereavement, such as the death of someone you love, which begins a process of mourning.

- The loss of something significant to you, such as a relationship, job or ambition.

Loss is broader than bereavement. Although types of loss can be very different, similar emotions arise for many people.

Grief is the loudest silence I have ever heard.

Angie Cartwright

What might cause grief?

The loss of anything that matters to you, whether tangible or intangible, can cause grief emotions. While the death of a loved one is possibly the most obvious cause of grief, it can also be caused by:

- Loss of a friendship or romantic relationship.

- Loss of a job or role.

- Loss of good health and/or mobility.

- Loss of a baby through miscarriage.

- Loss of a pet.

- Loss of a personal ambition.

- Loss or theft of a valuable possession.

- Loss of self-confidence or respect from others.

- Loss of feeling safe due to a traumatic event.

- Loss of freedom.

Finding your way

In reality, grief is not a straightforward process with a clear start and end point like this:

Grief is more like this, a messy, unpredictable experience without a clear ending:

We are all different. How you experience grief and express it will be unique to you. The timescale will be unique, as will how you find your way through it. Your learning and growth from the experience will be personal to you. You are a human, not a robot.

TO FEEL GRIEF IS

TO BE HUMAN

Myths

Unfortunately, there are many myths and misunderstandings about grief. These can cause hurt and shame and can make grieving last longer and feel harder than it could otherwise be.

Myth	Truth
Grieving means there's something wrong with you	Grieving is an entirely natural and normal reaction to loss
Grieving is a sign of weakness	To grieve is to grow
Time heals	Time helps, but you need accurate information and help from others too
You should avoid negative or unpleasant feelings	Your feelings are valid, whatever they may be
You should keep quiet about the loss	You may choose to have privacy, but your grief does not have to be a secret

Emotional and physical symptoms

Feelings are experienced in two parts: subjective emotions (such as sadness) and physical sensations (such as a racing heartbeat). You might pay more attention to one than the other, yet both are impacted by grief.

Emotional symptoms when experiencing grief often include:

- Feeling withdrawn.
- Being unable to concentrate, always thinking about the loss.
- Feeling like, "What's the point?"
- Feeling angry about the loss.
- Experiencing panic attacks.
- Feeling like it's your fault.
- Feeling unhappy for long stretches of time.

Grief is not just "a feeling" – it impacts your whole body, including your heart muscles, gut and kidneys. It also affects the fibrinogen levels in your liver, which cause blood clotting. Physical symptoms of grief often include:

- Physical numbness.

- Stomach pain and reduced appetite.

- Feeling exhausted.

- Aching muscles, headaches and neck tension.

- Lowered immunity.

- Chest pain, as if your heart feels broken.

- Feeling tight in the throat when trying to speak about the loss.

Although all these symptoms are normal to experience in the aftermath of a loss event, if they do not reduce after six months then this might indicate the need for professional help. Contact your doctor if you experience any severe physical symptoms.

How grief impacts your brain

The physical absence of someone or something significant to you will change the chemistry in your brain, which has a knock-on effect in every cell of your body.

Dopamine is the brain chemical that helps you to feel desire and motivation and to feel capable of action. Grief reduces dopamine, causing low mood and feelings of boredom and irritation. Grief elevates stress hormones such as cortisol and corticotropin releasing factor (known as CRF), affecting parts of the brain that regulate sleep, body temperature and appetite, as well as the adrenal glands above the kidneys. These stress hormones help to mobilize the body, but too much impairs the immune system.

There is a chemical reason why experiencing grief can cause feelings of isolation. Grief can block oxytocin, the brain chemical known for feelings of attachment, nurture and warmth, which is often activated through human touch, listening to music you enjoy and stroking a pet. Grief impacts the amount of serotonin in your brain, the brain chemical which generates feelings of well-being and optimism and stabilizes moods. Exposure to sunlight is a natural way to increase serotonin levels, as well as brisk walking and looking at cherished souvenirs and photographs.

Origins of "grief"

The word grief has been in use for over 800 years. It comes from an Old French word *grever*, which means to burden or oppress. In turn this came from the Latin word *gravare*, meaning "to make heavy". Grief can be traced to other words such as grave, gravity and aggrieved. The history of the word is a reminder of how grief can feel physically – like a weight pulling you down.

Endings

Sometimes endings are gradual and you can work toward them, like changing jobs or graduating from university. However, sometimes endings can feel sudden and traumatic. Divorce might bring an unexpected end to financial security, access to children or damage your social status. Moving home might not only mark a physical ending, but it can trigger grief emotions if it severs you from emotional attachments, bringing an end to all that was familiar.

Endings can arouse mixed feelings, not only bringing a change in practical circumstances but also changing how you perceive yourself.

Attending to your grief

Whatever the loss event – whether a bereavement or significant change in your circumstances or status – grief needs to be noticed and named, rather than brushed aside. It can be noticed emotionally through the experience of it in your body, such as turmoil, sadness or weight, as well as mentally, such as hectic thoughts and trying to make sense of what has occurred.

Grief will not submit to a timetable or wait until you have more time. Grief illuminates your attachment to life itself. To attend to your grief is to acknowledge and honour the presence of love.

I AM NOT

MY GRIEF;

I AM GRIEVING

Confusion

Many people say experiencing loss is like feeling lost. The resulting grief can feel "dark", "heavy", "foggy" as if entering a nowhere zone between the old version of life and the new. Remember, something significant has happened to you. Although unpleasant and frustrating, it is normal for sleep patterns to get turned upside down, leading you to feel wide awake at night and exhausted during the day. Forgetting basic things and struggling to finish sentences is also common. The underlying feeling is, "Where am I?" This can be upsetting and unsettling, but it will usually pass.

Mixed feelings

Grief includes a wide range of emotions which often conflict, such as feeling tremendous sadness at the loss yet possibly some relief, anger, serenity or even optimism. This might sound strange but the loss may bring an end to suffering, long-standing frustration or uncertainty. Conflicting feelings can be confusing – "Should I really feel this way?" or, "Am I a bad person for feeling so resentful?" Grief is complicated. Mixed feelings are not unusual. You don't need to over analyze your reaction or replay events over and over, just let it be what it is. Be gentle toward your experience.

Grief is love not wanting to let go.

Earl A. Grollman

Background loss

During any transition, grief emotions are likely to arise. Even positive changes can trigger anxiety or sadness. Starting university, achieving a promotion or beginning a new relationship may feel exciting but there may be "background losses", such as the comfort of a morning routine, travelling particular routes or seeing familiar faces. If you overlook these losses, they can cause difficulties later on. If you recognize what the "background losses" might be, you may be able to minimize their impact. For example, by setting clear boundaries, continuing a hobby which replenishes you or agreeing to keep in contact with someone.

Global events

Grief emotions may be triggered by overwhelming global events, such as the climate crisis. The loss of biodiversity and environmental habitats impacts day-to-day life. Everything you buy, wear, eat and drink has been extracted from the natural environment. Philosopher Glenn Albrecht named this type of grief "solstalgia" – the feeling of your natural home being threatened. This might stir intense emotions such as a desire to protest, anxiety about your future or feeling powerless. You might consider joining with others to take positive action. However personal or global the grief, focus on what you can do, not what you can't.

Expectations

Unmet expectations can become a source of grief, especially after a significant change, such as a change of job, home or relationship. Unspoken expectations can cause excitement to turn to disappointment, confusion and possibly anger. "I didn't expect it to be quite like this," is a common phrase after a major change in circumstances. To reduce the chances of this in the future, consider writing down your expectations and what these are based on. Could you communicate your expectations with others and listen to what others expect too? You could prevent some unintended grief occurring.

Grief is the feeling of reaching out for someone who has always been there, only to find that when you need them one more time, they are no longer there.

———

Anonymous

Dealing with stigma

Some types of grief are harder to talk openly about because of social prejudice. The ending of a same-sex relationship may receive less sympathy than if it were opposite-sex partners. The death of someone from suicide or the loss of a baby through miscarriage sometimes carries a stigma, as if these things shouldn't happen. And yet they are a devastating reality and it is essential to talk about them. Grief is grief. Nobody else decides who or what matters to you. The more we understand all the ways we encounter grief, the more compassionate we become toward one another.

When grief gets stuck

It can be tempting to ignore your grief and just get on with things, but this can impact you emotionally and physically in the longer-term. Research by the American Psychological Association explains how unresolved grief can affect the immune system, cause aches in the body, frequent fatigue and increase the risk of depression.

Indications you may be avoiding facing the loss you experienced include:

- If you abruptly change the conversation whenever someone mentions a similar type of loss, or something that reminds you of the loss.

- You do not or cannot talk about the loss without there being a strong reaction in your body, such as trembling or your muscles going rigid.

- It feels painful when you recall positive memories of the person or situation.

- Your mind revisits the loss, time and time again. This suggests that it wants your attention and needs talking through with someone you can trust.

- You spend considerable time keeping "busy" and never rest properly.

The pain of grief will remain strong in your body if you do not face your loss. Later in the book we will discuss ways to understand and accept grief as part of your recovery.

You are not alone

Grief looks and feels different for everyone, but remember you are not alone in the experience of it. There are many ways that you might encounter loss – whether through bereavement, a significant change in health or an unexpected event. Although it is impossible to predict precisely when grief might occur and how it might impact you, you are human and your experience of it will be valid. You can let go of thinking it should be "like this" or "like that". Grief is the flip side of love, something which unites us all.

People talk about grief as emptiness, but it's not empty. It's full. Heavy. Not an absence to fill.

Elan Mastai

How
do we
grieve?

Recognizing loss

Sometimes it may be difficult to recognize loss has occurred. You may have hurried on with your life and not realized the impact of losing someone or something important to you that is no longer present or possible. You may have a nagging sense of grief: "I used to be able to just..." or, "I remember when...". Be gentle with yourself. Life is always changing. Perhaps now is a chance to change something and recover what mattered to you. Or maybe it is time to let go and grieve what could have been but is no more.

The ball in the bucket

A metaphor: Think of your mind as a bucket and grief as a ball. When the loss event first happens, the grief is like a huge ball filling the entire bucket leaving no room to think of anything except the grief. It seems like it will always be like this. But slowly the ball shrinks, from the size of a basketball to the size of a volleyball, a tennis ball, then a golf ball. The grief doesn't matter less, but gradually there is more room to function mentally. The grief doesn't disappear; it becomes part of your life experience.

**Embrace your grief.
For there, your
soul will grow.**

———————

Carl Jung

Weight of the world

Be careful if you hear yourself using the word "should" when considering how you grieve. "Should" suggests you must do something in a certain way or at a certain time to keep someone else happy, perhaps to prevent you from feeling guilty or resentful toward others. The "shoulds" in your mind will rest heavily on your shoulders.

Remember: You have choices. Be clear about what is your responsibility and what is not. Swap the word "should" for "could". Ask yourself: "What could I do to honour the loss? What would I like to do?" How does it feel to choose?

Upbringing

A powerful influence on how you respond to grief will be the role models you had as a child: parents, grandparents, teachers and other authority figures. As a child you observed, listened to and copied others' words and behaviours. Psychologists call this process "introjection" – taking on the beliefs and habits of others without consciously choosing them.

Who from the past influences your present response to grief? Does it help or hinder you now? For example: "Grandma went for a quiet walk each evening, but dad told me off if I cried." Give yourself permission to grieve differently to them.

I WILL BE

PATIENT WITH

MY GRIEF

You don't have to...

When grieving, remember:

- You do not have to "move on"
  to keep anyone else happy.

- You do not have to "get over it".

- You do not have to "put it all behind you".

- You do not have to "put a brave face on".

- You do not have to "prove how strong
  you are".

Grief is hard enough as it is without taking on
other people's lack of compassion or patience.

We are all different

No two people will experience grief in the same way. Regardless of gender, ethnicity, sexual orientation, age, culture and mobility, there is no right or wrong way to grieve. Grieving is as unique as your fingerprints. Some people experience certain aspects of grief more strongly than others. You may find you ruminate more, which means getting caught up in repetitive, negative and introspective thoughts about a loss. Or you might occupy yourself with always keeping busy. Both these reactions to grief are common. It is important to notice what you do and the impact of this on your energy levels.

Denial is the shock absorber for the soul... It wards off the blows of life until we can gather our other coping resources.

Melody Beattie

Phases of grief

You may have heard of "the five stages of grief" (denial; anger; bargaining; depression; acceptance) – a model developed by Swiss-American psychiatrist Elisabeth Kübler-Ross in 1969, which is often used when talking about grief. Kübler-Ross explained her work was specifically about death and dying from a terminal illness, not general loss. Although grief may not unfold in such a staged way, the model can offer the vocabulary to express what you are feeling at different points in time, which itself may provide comfort. But don't worry about squeezing your experience into a theory.

As you grieve, your emotions may happen in phases, but there is no timetable to grief. Certain emotions such as anger or sadness might become emphasized at certain times and you may not be sure why. Grief is not a solid object. Rather than thinking of fixed stages of grief, like a staircase, it may be useful to consider grief emotions having phases like waves that come and go. Remember: there are no absolute certainties that grief will be like this or like that. Grief is a fluid process which, when noticed and named, can gradually lead to acceptance and growth.

Shock

The first emotion that may occur in the immediate aftermath of a loss, before denial, is shock. The feeling of shock can be so strong it causes you to think you are unable to cope. But shock emotions, such as anxiety, panic and fear, are communicating a vital message: you need to feel safe again and find ways to cope with the situation. Shock emotions are a strong reminder to find a safe place and give yourself a chance to regain some control, even if it is just over your breathing and ability to communicate what you need to someone else.

Denial

It is common immediately after a loss to feel cut off from everyone, as if in a bubble with real life continuing without you. You might think, "Is this happening?" or, "It can't be true." Denial, as a response to loss, is not wrong. It is an unconscious way of protecting yourself from experiencing too many emotions at one time. Denial differs from acceptance. With denial you are more likely to say "I'm fine". With acceptance, talking about the loss has a softness to it. Denial is useful in the short-term, but eventually grief does have to be faced.

GRIEF DOES NOT

ARRIVE WITH

AN END DATE

ATTACHED

Bargaining

Your mind might wrestle with the facts of a loss, trying to resolve what happened. You might attempt to bargain with a higher power in an attempt to alleviate the pain of grief or to try to change the situation. For instance: "If you help me, then I promise to...". Positive bargaining means taking a risk to help yourself. It may lead you to try out a new coping strategy ("If I try this, then I might feel better"), make a new request ("If I say what I need, then I might be heard") or make an important decision ("If I forgive them, then I can move on").

Anger and aggression

Anger is a natural, valid and healthy response to loss. If you are grieving the loss of a loved one, you may feel angry with them for leaving you, or with someone else for not preventing it. If a relationship or job ending was not your choosing, anger might start to emerge once the reality of the loss hits you. The loss might affect intangible things like your self-respect, safety and status. You might think, "Why me?" or, "What have I done to deserve this?" Remember: anger is not aggression. Anger is the body's response to loss; aggression is the unsafe physical expression of anger. Speak your anger safely, do not act it out unsafely. Showing aggression toward others only triggers more loss, to those around you and yourself.

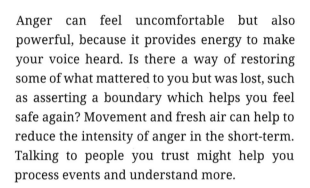

Anger can feel uncomfortable but also powerful, because it provides energy to make your voice heard. Is there a way of restoring some of what mattered to you but was lost, such as asserting a boundary which helps you feel safe again? Movement and fresh air can help to reduce the intensity of anger in the short-term. Talking to people you trust might help you process events and understand more.

If we do not know how to mourn, we cannot know how to live.

_____

Peter Marris

Depression

Feeling low for weeks on end indicates you have reached your limit for now and may be starting to feel the reality of the loss, although putting words to it may seem impossible. Life may feel meaningless. "What's the point?" you might say. Depression is different to sadness. Sadness typically occurs in short waves and has times of respite afterward, whereas depression is a persistent low mood with little capacity for humour or joy. Depression is often made worse by rumination. You might not cry at all and just feel pulled to the ground. The gravity of grief changes you.

Acceptance

Accepting the loss has happened does not mean you are "over" it. You may feel sadness regarding a significant loss for many years. Eventually, although you may still feel sad at remembering what was, you adapt and start to rebuild your life. The past has gone, but a different future opens up. Accepting how the loss has changed your life is important, realizing that life will never go back to how it was. At first, acceptance may simply mean more good days than bad ones. This is okay. The grief journey happens one day at a time.

JUST AS THE

WAVES IN AN

OCEAN CHANGE, SO

DO MY EMOTIONS

When a wave of grief hits, it can feel overwhelming. Hold on; you will resurface.

Zoë Clark-Coates

Noticing and naming

It might be tempting to hide emotions that are painful, confusing or frightening. However, if you push your emotions away, denying that they are there, they will just find another way of showing up. This might be as tension in the body, over-the-top reactions in your behaviour or making hurtful remarks. You do not have to wear your heart on your sleeve nor update everyone on social media every day, but a simple protective step for yourself (and others around you) will be to notice and name your emotions.

Making sense of emotions

Emotions are not good or bad, right or wrong, positive or negative. They tend to be pleasant, neutral or unpleasant. We generally prefer pleasant ones. Because grief impacts the way the human brain works, pleasant emotions such as happiness, optimism and gratitude are likely to be in short supply when you are grieving.

Your body is a mirror to your mind. Learning to bring more awareness to the sensations happening inside your body will help you "name" the feelings you experience. Naming feelings creates distance between "you" (the person) and "it" (the experience). After all, you are not just a brain floating in the air full of thoughts, your whole body is involved in experiencing life on earth.

Emotion words often linked to loss include:

Shock	Denial	Anger	Guilt
Numb Dread Confused Overwhelmed Panicky	Forgetting about the loss Feeling stuck Hiding yourself away	Furious Bitter Resentful Out of control	Regretful Torn Ashamed Self-blame

Depression	Bargaining	Acceptance
Alone Powerless Empty Heart-broken	Trying to change something Fantasizing Taking a risk Seeking help	Sad but okay Letting go Serene Relieved

Short fuse

Do not be surprised if you feel irritated more quickly. Tiny things like a spilled drink or being late might trigger an over-the-top angry reaction to someone close to you. This can be shocking: "I didn't think I was the sort of person who yelled!" Grieving steals your capacity to be patient. If you do overreact, do not make it worse by punishing yourself. You are more than your behaviour. How can you repair the situation? Perhaps have a kind word with yourself: "I am grieving. This is hard. I need to rest." Grief does not require immaculate behaviour.

Values

Emotions are not random events, although when and how they show up may surprise you. This might be embarrassing if you burst into tears in a shop or overreact to a stranger. Grief emotions can be like the weather and shift unexpectedly. Your emotions reveal your values, indicating who and what matters to you. Whatever your values are, that is where a range of loss emotions such as anxiety, frustration and sadness, are likely to arise. Ask yourself: "Who and what really matters to me?" List your values. Notice how emotions are harnessed to what you care about.

Crying

"Why am I crying all the time?" and, "Why aren't I crying?" are both normal questions immediately after a loss. Sometimes you need to let tears come, without force, if they want to. Crying releases stress hormones such as cortisol that can build up in the body and cause physical and emotional tension. Crying restores the brain's ability to think clearly. However, crying does not mean you are weak and not crying does not mean you do not feel pain. You may have other ways of showing emotion. Grief changes you, so you may exhibit different responses to what you expect.

What we have once enjoyed we can never lose, for all that we love deeply becomes a part of us.

Helen Keller

How
to cope with
grief

Keep routines

Although grief is incredibly painful, there are small positive steps you can take that can help to prevent you from feeling overwhelmed. One healthy way to cope is keeping a daily routine: having a shower or bath, getting dressed and doing other basics like brushing your teeth, even if you are not leaving the house. You will feel better for the bit of effort it requires. Maintaining some patterns of "normal life" can carry you through the hardest days. There is comfort and safety in routine.

It takes courage to get out of bed in the morning and climb into the day.

———————

Edward Hirsch

Taking care of your mind and your body

If you feel physically healthy, you will cope better emotionally and mentally. Here is a checklist for your daily physical well-being.

S – Sleep
H – Hydration
E – Exercise
D – Diet

On a scale of 0–10, where 10 is "great", what score would you give yourself for each of these today? This is not an exam. A low number is okay. The aim is not to score "10" for each one, but to consider what you can do to help each one go up by one or two points today. The following tips offer some ideas.

Bedtime

Grief is exhausting, so you might sleep at different times to what was normal for you before the loss. Consider having a routine such as a fixed bedtime. Turn off any screens at least an hour before you go to bed, lower the room lighting and change into your bed clothes. These simple actions help stimulate the natural hormone melatonin, which helps create that "sleepy feeling". Consider having a bright lamp on in the mornings to stimulate the hormone serotonin and feelings of wakefulness. Although these steps will not guarantee you a good night's sleep, they will provide structure for better rest.

Hydration

Drink plenty of water. Aim for about 1.5 litres (2½ pints) a day or eight small glasses, depending on the weather and the amount of exercise you do. Not only does drinking water avoid dehydration (which would cause headaches, tiredness and constipation), it also increases the brain's temperature and gets rid of toxins and dead cells. If your brain feels "too full" to remember doing this, put a note somewhere obvious giving yourself instructions: "DRINK WATER". Yes, it may sound daft, but basic choices each day create stability. Good hydration is self-care and will strengthen you in the context of your recovery.

EACH DAY IS

A NEW DAY

Harmful ways of coping

Excessive alcohol consumption, use of certain drugs and gambling can all become harmful ways of coping. Alcohol is perhaps the most socially acceptable, yet it is a depressant, preventing the body absorbing an amino acid called tryptophan which has a vital role in regulating mood. Overconsumption is an easy trap to fall into when your willpower feels low and you are looking to lift your mood, but it will not help you grieve or adjust to the loss in the long run. If you find yourself getting into a pattern of addictive behaviour, then you must ask for help.

Nutrition

Eating different coloured fruit and vegetables will give your body a range of nutrients and reduce your blood pressure. Boost your energy levels and immune system by eating beans, leafy greens, nuts, seeds and wholegrain foods, which all provide magnesium. Go steady on potato-based products, which are slow to digest and will make you feel sluggish. Eat breakfast, even if it is small, as it gets your metabolism working more effectively. Keep washed fruit where you can see it, and make extra portions of meals which can be frozen for days when you don't want to cook.

Sometimes, carrying on, just carrying on, is the superhuman achievement.

Albert Camus

Safe places

Safe places can provide comfort and help restore your resilience to keep going on the hard days. Safe places can be relational, physical and mental.

- A relational safe place is someone with whom you feel at ease. Think about who won't judge you for how you are feeling, and who will stop what they are doing to listen to you. Just talking to someone you trust and letting them know how you really feel can help you get through a difficult day. There might be a certain author or poet whose writing comforts you too.

- Physical safe places could include certain parts of your home, such as a favourite armchair, your bedroom (just don't hide under the duvet for too long!) or your garden, if you have one. The countryside might offer a variety of safe places (more so in the daytime) which lift your spirits. Perhaps you feel safe visiting a favourite café or park with a friend.

- Mental safe places might include gazing at the sky, cherishing a memory or holding a physical object that brings feelings of connection. Some people find comfort creating a "memory box" of photographs and souvenirs that remind them of a person or place.

Continuing

It can be tricky knowing what to say when someone asks, "How are you coping?" Maybe you want to skip the conversation entirely or feel a pressure to reassure them you are okay. But your process is about you, not them. Having a response prepared in advance can buy you time as you decide how much you want to say, if anything at all. Examples include: "I'm continuing, and that's good enough," or, "I've got something to focus on today." In many western cultures talking about loss still feels socially awkward. That's not your fault!

Turn to friends and family

Grief often creates feelings of loneliness because it takes up so much energy and can be intensely personal. This is normal, but do not isolate yourself. You may have taken pride in being self-sufficient before, but now is the time to lean on those who care about you. Spend time with them, rather than avoiding them. Accept help – be it a listening ear, a meal or simply a hug. If someone reaches out to you it is because they care. Be open to help in the same way you would want others to be open to your help.

THOUGHTS ARE

NOT FACTS

One thing at a time

Life can feel overwhelming when you are grieving. Focusing on one day at a time can help you cope with your feelings and get through everyday tasks that you need to do. You may need to take things more slowly than usual, or you may need to start a new activity that gives your mind a break. Do what works best for you. You won't always have energy, but you do have a choice.

**Take one day at a time.
Or one hour at a time.**

Even just one moment at a time is enough – it really is.

Talk to people
who understand

It may not be your closest loved ones you turn to. Could you find a support group of people in your local area, in person or online, who can identify with your particular type of loss? Try it once and see if it helps; trust your instincts. It might be a place where you can just listen, be among others who understand something about what you are experiencing and not have to pretend everything is fine. Sharing your sorrow with others who have experienced similar losses can help create healing bonds and the strength to continue.

Grit your teeth and let it hurt. Don't deny it, don't be overwhelmed by it. It will not last forever.

———————

Harold Kushner

Mindfulness

Grief can generate repetitive patterns of negative "what if" thinking. Practising mindfulness can help to ease ruminating trains of thought that might be heightening your anxiety.

Mindfulness practice is thousands of years old and is relevant for persons of any faith or none. It is simply the practice of paying attention to the moment or experience without labelling it as "good" or "awful".

Pausing and noticing moments during the day can give you "mental oxygen", lowering your blood pressure, strengthening your immune system and providing much-needed rest. Best of all, mindfulness is free and does not require complicated equipment or formal training.

Mindfulness includes:

- Paying attention to the flow of your breath.

- Using natural sound as a focal point, such as birdsong or water.

- Noticing your body sensations and detecting any tension from the top of your head to your feet.

You might tend to resist or cling to painful emotions, and while both responses are valid, this only makes them feel stronger and last longer. Instead, when strong emotions appear, notice the physical sensations and breathe in. Say, "Here it is" to the emotion. Then breathe out. Accept what is happening. Ride the wave, knowing it will pass.

Make a "loss list"

Creating a "loss list" can help you identify different aspects of a loss. Ask yourself, "What will change (or has changed) as a result of this specific loss?" Mentally go through your day and write down what has gone, including the intangible aspects. Perhaps write the list over the course of a week. The important thing is to become aware of what has been lost to you. Naming specific losses can help you to either accept them (if you cannot get them back) or, if a loss is within your control, you may be able to do something to restore it.

"When I... then I..."

Creating new habits is hard enough at the best of times but they can help you cope by providing a routine. To make forming habits easier, identify a specific thing you already do every day, such as cleaning your teeth, boiling a kettle or feeding the cat. This provides a concrete base on which to experiment with a new habit. Keep it simple and specific.

Examples include:

When I boil the kettle... then I will say three things I am grateful for.

When I get into bed... then I will read a book which lifts my mood.

I AM MORE THAN

MY FEELINGS

Practise feelings of safety

Loss experiences may cause you to get caught up in abstract thoughts about the past and future. One way to anchor yourself in the present moment is to orientate yourself in your immediate physical environment. Make a list of:

1. Five safe things you can see (notice colours, light, views through windows).

2. Five safe things you can hear (notice background sounds, like a clock or birdsong).

3. Five safe things you can hold (notice comforting and solid objects where you are).

Feeling safe and present requires practice. Sensations are always available to ground yourself in the here and now.

You have within you,
right now, everything
you need to deal with
whatever the world
can throw at you.

Brian Tracy

3–4–5 breathing

Your breath is a source of help in times of distress. Regulating your breathing has an instant positive effect on your heart rate and blood pressure, calming the part of the brain which reacts when feeling threatened.

Use this 3–4–5 process to regulate your breathing:

1. Press your feet into the ground.

2. Breathe in through your nose and count to three (notice your shoulders rise).

3. Hold your breath in your chest for a count of four (notice a feeling of control).

4. Breathe out a long breath through your mouth, count to five (notice how nice a long breath feels).

5. Repeat five times.

Boundaries

It is vital to have boundaries because your emotions can be triggered by who and what is in your immediate environment. It is okay to say "no" to invitations if you do not have the energy. Rather than ignoring the message, thank them for the invite and give your reason up front: "Thanks, but I just don't have the energy right now." Most people will respect this. Your friends are not telepathic, so say what you can and cannot manage. Use "I/my" messages, not "you/your" messages. For example: "I need a night off," or, "My body needs rest," rather than, "You always pester me," or, "Why don't you leave me alone?" Do not let feeling low contaminate your communication.

Managing your environment is important, too. Consider turning off television channels or blocking certain websites that are likely to trigger your mood, such as news websites. You might want to place a "Do not disturb" sign on your door. Decide on what times you can be available for others. If mornings are especially hard, can you delay certain tasks or contact people after lunch? Grief will not obey your calendar, but you must "guard your energy". Grief is exhausting.

Everyday soundtrack

One way to give the "thinking brain" a rest is to focus on external sounds. Sounds are not thoughts. They shift your attention from an internal analytic process to the outside world. Listen to background sounds such as your footsteps, the clunk of unlocking the door, the click of putting the kettle on, the whoosh of water gushing from the tap. Notice the constant everyday soundtrack to your day. Rather than labelling or analyzing the sounds, let them remind you that life continues.

Gratitude

You may think, "What is there to be thankful for?" when faced with a significant loss. You don't need to pretend all is well. Yet, even in painful circumstances, there will be simple things to be grateful for: Hearing a bird sing. An act of kindness. Warmth, food and shelter. Focus on what you do have, rather than what you don't.

Notice specific, sensory things.
Notice what is going well.
Notice who helps.

Practising gratitude each day reduces stress hormones elevated by grief and improves memory, attention and decision making.

Swearing

Do not be surprised if you speak negatively to yourself, either in your head or out loud, more than usual. Swearing more often is typical when feeling the strain and stress of loss. You might be thinking, "I should be able to deal with this better." Give yourself permission to swear in a room on your own, or outdoors, or with others who are comfortable with this behaviour. Use whatever words you want, especially the ones others wouldn't approve of. Swearing out loud (in a safe place) can release internal tension.

Others' reactions

If your grief emotions seem to make others feel uncomfortable, that is not your responsibility. Remember, they might be on their own grief journey too. Your circle of friendships might shrink for a while but do not take this as rejection. There is nothing wrong with you. The "grieving you" may not need a massive social life for a while. Be careful how you invest your time and energy, because grief is hard work. While you do not have to be busy, you might want to keep certain regular activities going that keep you tethered to the real world.

Sometimes it's okay if the only thing you did today was breathe.

Yumi Sakugawa

Living
with
grief

Hope heals

There is no formula about how to live with and through grief. You do not have to create a complicated recovery plan or "get it right". Even minor losses, which cause disappointment, can undermine your energy and rob you of a decent night's sleep. Living with grief means staying open to hope. Being hopeful does not mean being naive nor pretending everything is fine. It is about using your will to help yourself and express your experience, despite the pain or temptation to give up. Notice which of the following suggestions bring you relief and offer glimmers of hope.

Listen to your body

You can't make grief disappear by being busy, but having constructive things to do after a loss might give you focus, purpose and a sense of progress. However, be careful about squashing your grief emotions. Listen to your body. Ask yourself, "How am I feeling, right now?" For example, if you are experiencing frequent headaches, muscle tension or stomach problems your body may be saying it needs rest, care or a medical check-up. Unless, little by little, you allow yourself to face grief and express it, it will remain. Listening to your body opens the door to hope and recovery.

You will survive and will find purpose in the chaos. Moving on doesn't mean letting go.

Mary VanHaute

Avoidance

You might want to avoid certain people, places and activities after a loss. This often happens and is a normal way to protect yourself from embarrassment or to preserve energy. But avoiding them for too long makes it harder to return to aspects of life that hold meaning and interest for you.

Consider these questions:

- Who are you avoiding?

- What places are you avoiding?

- What activities are you avoiding?

For each of these, what are you frightened might happen if you stopped avoiding them?

Beginning with the easiest, what is a small positive step you could take to reduce avoidance?

Relate to grief

If grief were a person, how would you relate to them? Perhaps at first you would want to ignore them, then maybe shout at them? After a while you might realize that grief is present. Eventually, you might welcome grief with curiosity and give it your attention. Ask the grief what it wants to show you. The dynamic between you and your grief might then change. Sometimes the grief might be dominant, other times it might be dormant. Whatever your changing relationship with grief, you may begin to hold an underlying respect for its presence which has something to teach you.

I DON'T HAVE TO

GET OVER IT

BUT I WILL GET

THROUGH IT

Be patient

Be patient with grief – there is no shortcut. Tonkin's model of grief suggests some people don't experience the grief getting "smaller" but instead as a person they grow around their grief. The grief stays as significant as the first day of loss, but in time, the intensity of the sadness eases and you begin to feel relief and moments of joy alongside grief. You will adjust to your new circumstances at your own pace. You may want to hurry up and "get there" but it doesn't work that way. Be patient. You are growing. You will make it through.

Notice how far you have come

Take stock of your progress since your loss. The brain easily reverts to survival mode, narrowing its focus to what still needs to improve. Press pause, look back and notice what you have coped with and what challenges you have already come through. Rather than relegating your resilience to the distant past, remind yourself today of what you have learned and discovered. The paradox of grief is that it can also generate gratitude. Perhaps you slow down and appreciate your life more, or empathize with others more because of what you have experienced. Take a moment to notice.

Milestones

When grieving, it is normal for some days to be more difficult than others. These might be special occasions such as birthdays, an anniversary, Christmas or attending an event that might trigger intense emotion. The stress and worry of an upcoming milestone can feel worse than the day itself. Milestones are hard to navigate because elements of them will not necessarily be in your control. Your emotions may not follow a particular pattern or show up in the way you expect. They are like the weather – sometimes the forecast is wrong.

The first milestone occasions following the loss will usually be the hardest just because the memories will be most recent. You may experience conflicting emotions: sadness, remembrance, self-pity and perhaps a desire to move forward in some way. If you have experienced a bereavement, you can prepare for feeling grief more intensely on "celebration" days. Can you speak to someone about your worries? Is there anything practical you can put in place? Remember: such occasions can also provide comfort, so be open to this possibility.

It takes strength
to make your way
through grief, to grab
hold of life and let it
pull you forward.

———————

Patti Davis

Remembering

There are positive actions you can take to preserve memories of events or people, such as planting a tree, donating to a favourite organization in memory of a loved one or making a memory box. If it is not a bereavement but the ending of a particular life stage (such as university or retirement), maybe there are cards, photographs or souvenirs you want to keep on display. How you choose to remember a person or experience is up to you. Do not feel pressured to memorialize in a certain way. Do what feels healthy and uplifting for you.

Create a memory book or box

One way of remembering a person (or perhaps a certain event) is to create a physical memory book (or box). You could involve family members or close friends if you would like to, or do this alone. Gather together photos, newspaper cuttings and bigger items – anything that is meaningful to you and tells something of the story you want to keep alive. This could be favourite films, songs, places, sayings, a cherished watch, fabric, scent or sports item. There is no need to do this in one go: take your time and go through the process at your own pace.

If you want to include other people's memories of your loved one (or significant event), send a message to relevant people inviting them to contribute a fond memory, photo or story of how the person (or event) enriched their life. This process can bring new stories to light and be a wonderful insight for children or grandchildren.

Collate the messages in a large scrapbook or photo album (perhaps online) whose design has positive associations for you, or physical items in a decorated shoebox. It is entirely up to you how you arrange items, whether by theme or as a timeline.

MY GRIEF
MATTERS;
MY GROWTH
MATTERS TOO

What about medication?

Grief is not an illness. Do not assume you need antidepressants or other medication. Medication may help in the short term to relieve symptoms of grief but it cannot take the grief away. Medication itself cannot teach coping strategies or help you grow through grief, and some medications may have undesirable side effects, such as causing sleep disruption, weight gain, headaches and nausea. However, if intense grief makes it hard to function in your daily life, then there is a risk this can lead to clinical depression. In this case, seeking the advice of your doctor is certainly recommended.

Complicated grief

Grief is a natural response to any kind of loss. However, sometimes normal grief emotions do not lessen in the way you expect and the pain stays at an intense level, as if the loss has only just happened even though it is months later. Grief can then become more complicated, which can lead to a grief disorder. If you or someone close to you is struggling to cope, do reach out for professional and experienced help (see the Resources section at the end of this book). Seeking help is itself a sign of strength and desire to heal.

THERE IS LIFE

AFTER GRIEF

Professional help

Sometimes those close to you will be affected by the same loss. Despite their best intentions, they cannot be unbiased. Consider speaking with a qualified therapist, someone without an agenda offering you a safe, supportive space to think or talk through whatever is on your mind. The process of talking openly about grief increases blood flow to parts of the brain responsible for organizing and decision-making. Remember that accessing therapy does not mean there is anything that needs "fixing". Receiving support is a sign of courage, whether to make some sense of your experience or to develop coping strategies.

Hope is being able
to see that there
is light despite all
of the darkness.

Desmond Tutu

Journaling

Journaling is the practice of keeping a written account of what you are thinking or feeling about certain relationships or situations, positive or negative. It is a physical way of processing the tangle of thoughts and feelings generated by grief. Moving your hand along the page (or the keypad) can give your mind a focal point. Thoughts don't come with punctuation, whereas words sit still on the page so you can notice what you are thinking. Then you can close the journal and decide, "That's done for now." One benefit is that over time your journal will show you how far you have come on your grief journey.

Make up your own journaling rules: write, doodle, draw, use blank or lined pages. To get started, find a notebook (or app) you like the look of. Perhaps find a pen or pencil that feels pleasant to hold so you will want to use it. Keep your journal somewhere safe but easy for you to reach. If you are not sure what to write, you could use sentence stems, such as:

- Today I noticed...

- Something that went well today was...

- In one word, my body feels...

- I am thankful for...

Take up an activity you enjoy

Choose a specific, positive activity you will commit to, perhaps going for a swim, being part of a book club or volunteering for an outdoors project. You know yourself best. This provides three sources of enjoyment:

- Firstly, the positive anticipation of looking forward to it.

- Secondly, the enjoyment of the actual activity.

- Thirdly, the satisfaction of having done it.

The activity itself might only occupy a few hours in your week but it can provide many more hours of mental relief and pleasure, helping you to cope with grief by doing things which restore motivation and generate well-being.

The power of "up yours"

Maybe some days (or weeks) the last thing you want will be a mushy sounding mindfulness technique, someone suggesting you journal or speaking to a professional helper. You won't feel like going for a walk, practising self-care or reading a book like this one. It might feel too smothering. You might just want to scream, swear, sob your heart out or have a "clearing out" frenzy. Let your life be messy for a while. You choose. Even this has power tucked inside it: the choice to say "up yours" or "screw this" to all the well-meaning advice.

Closure isn't always possible

Significant changes don't always cause grief and some types of loss may bring a clear sense of "closure", perhaps through a ceremony or physical separation, like moving home. But for many types of loss which do cause grief emotions discussed in this book, there may never be a feeling of "that's over and done with". Grief does not have a specific timeframe and won't necessarily come to a neat and tidy end. Perhaps consider grief as being like the roots of a tree going down, an ongoing process which in time helps you flourish.

We bereaved are not alone. We belong to the largest company in all the world – the company of those who have known suffering.

———————

Helen Keller

Supporting

others
who are
grieving

Be there

It can be difficult to know what to say or do when someone you care about is grieving after a loss. Knowing they are struggling with painful emotions can be tough. Initially, you may feel apprehensive about offering support because intense emotion can be so personal. You might feel uncomfortable, but do not let your own discomfort prevent you from reaching out to the other person. The most important thing you can do is be there for them. Your patient presence can be more comforting than any sentence you say.

You do not need to fix others

You may worry about saying the wrong thing to someone or not being able to find any words at all. This is natural; you do not need to fix them or give special advice. Do not search for a "magic wand". There isn't one. Your supportive presence could help more than you may ever know and small gestures can make the world of difference. There is power in just acknowledging the reality of a loss. Think about your own experience of loss. What has helped you in such times?

We rise by lifting others.

Robert Ingersoll

Create a climate of attention

A climate of attention means being at ease and letting someone else know that you notice them. It means dropping any judgement you have toward the other person. Nancy Kline, once awarded Listener of the Year by the International Listening Association, says that a climate of attention helps people think more clearly and freely. The components that do this include: ease, rather than rushing; appreciation, not criticism; equality, not dominance; allowing feelings to be expressed without judgement; and being in a place which says "you matter". Increasing any one of these aspects will improve the quality of attention you give.

Reach out

For some, the grieving starts after the ceremony is over (such as a funeral or leaving event) and a sense of reality sets in. This can be a lonely and empty place, as the early flood of support (such as replies to anything about the loss posted on social media) is replaced by mundane duties and ongoing tasks. Reach out during this time to check in with the person. Don't expect a phone call or text asking for your help; instead, be proactive. Affirm that you are there and that they are not forgotten.

YOUR QUIET

PRESENCE MAKES

A DIFFERENCE

Acknowledge the loss

When someone has experienced a loss, whether the death of a pet or a failed job interview, even just saying to them, "I'm sorry to hear that," can be a start. If you feel uncomfortable around grief, it may be tempting to cross the road to avoid conversation. Try not to do this, no matter how lost for words you may feel, as it can be hurtful and upsetting. Just saying something to acknowledge the loss can make a difference. Beneath all the drama, everyone deserves to be noticed and valued as a human being. Offer the gift of acknowledgement.

Listen with your heart

Grief is not intellectual. Researchers at the HeartMath Institute say that the human heart emits electromagnetic waves which can be detected up to 10 metres (33 feet) away. This is why you might sense a certain "vibe" when you walk into a room. Listening with an open heart and being unafraid to say what you notice is one of the most important things you can do to help someone grieving, whatever the type of loss. Acknowledge the other person's emotion regarding their loss, which you might see on their face, hear in their voice and sense in your own body.

Empathy is...
communicating that
incredibly healing
message of, "You
are not alone."

—————

Brené Brown

Empathy

An effective way of relieving grief for another person and helping to activate positive brain chemicals such as oxytocin and dopamine is to demonstrate empathy. This is not just "soft talk" or sympathy. Empathy means helping someone to really feel seen, heard and understood.
Ways of showing empathy include:

- Listening to the actual words someone uses to describe their grief.

- Not interrupting or rushing them.

- Responding thoughtfully, such as, "That sounds hard."

- Saying what you notice, such as, "You look tired."

- Admitting, "I can barely imagine what that might be like."

Consider how others have helped you feel "noticed". What did they do, or not do? What did they say? How did they say that? Draw on your own experience to bring wisdom and compassion into your interactions with others. However, be careful not to read too much into whether someone returns your eye contact or not when you speak with them. A lack of eye contact is not necessarily a sign of disinterest or disrespect. Some individuals find eye contact particularly uncomfortable. Empathy can be conveyed in many different ways, including body posture and your quality of attention.

Hold a space

It can be tempting to keep checking in with the other person to see how they are but do not smother them. They may not want to spend time with other people nor immediately acknowledge messages. Ask them directly what they need. Do they want company or some time alone? Striking a balance between reaching out and giving space is tricky, but letting them know you are thinking of them and that no response is required can be a sensitive way of showing you care.

The language of possibility

Avoid phrases suggesting inevitability, such as "You must feel…", "I bet you're feeling…" or "You will feel…". These suggest you are the expert on the other person's experience rather than them. The language of possibility means using more open-ended phrases such as "I imagine…", "I wonder if…", "might" and "perhaps", plus asking questions that convey empathy rather than assumption.

You could say:

- I imagine it might be hard for you right now.

- I'm wondering what you need this week?

- Can I help with something?

- Would you like to tell me what happened?

The hard question

Directly asking, "Would you like to tell me what happened?" may seem hard. It might go unanswered and yet the invitation to speak about a loss can help someone express what is of great value to them. One way in which the pain of grief leaves the body is through the lips, however clumsy or incomplete the words and sentences might sound. Speaking of a loss is to recognize what was, and what now is, honouring the love and loyalty that remains.

Be gentle

Try to avoid judgemental language when speaking to someone who is grieving because it will set them back in their recovery. Although the intensity of grief emotions usually change over time, it is unhelpful to say this to someone immediately after a loss event.

Judgemental phrases to avoid include:

- Never mind.

- You'll get over it.

- You shouldn't feel like that.

- That happened to me once.

- These things happen for a reason.

How to have a conversation about loss

Starting a conversation might be difficult, so use language which encourages openness. For example, if someone has lost a loved one, you could say something simple like, "I am so sorry to hear that (name) has died." By using the word "died" you are letting the person know that you are not avoiding what has happened. Even if it is not a bereavement, acknowledging the specific change in a situation creates frankness.

Imagine being in this person's situation. What might they be thinking? How might they be feeling? What might they need or want? You may not know for certain without asking them, but by considering the situation from their perspective, your conversation will naturally convey a tone of empathy.

Remember that grief is an intensely individual experience, so do not claim to "know" how the person is feeling or assume their grief experience is the same as yours. Loss emotions can change rapidly. Respect their thoughts and be prepared for them to swing between the depths of grief and the desire to get on with their life. Their moods may be changeable so go with the flow.

People will forget
what you said, people
will forget what you
did, but people will
never forget how you
made them feel.

Maya Angelou

Remember it's about them

Do not be offended if the other person turns down your offer of help or does not reply immediately to your message. They may feel "all over the place" and not know what support they want. Remove the pressure and give them a sense of agency by letting them know they can reply when it suits them. After all, this is about them, not you. Be mindful of what type of contact they might prefer. For example, some people might find text messages easier than speaking on the telephone; some may welcome a visit to their home, others may not.

Practical help

Offering to help someone in practical ways can be a relief for them, a reminder that they are not on their own. Here are some examples of ways to help:

- Cook a meal you know they would like (perhaps for their freezer).

- Do some housework or offer to watch their children for them.

- Shop for essentials they need.

- Give them lifts to where they need to go.

- Walk their dog (if they have one).

Do what you say you will do. Be specific and consistent. It will be a relief for them to know that you are willing to help rather than waiting to be asked.

Wish them well

Phrases like "sending you love" and "you are in my thoughts" do not have to be empty sentiments. Thoughts and emotions contain energy and impact other people. They won't change the past, but they do create a real dynamic in which recovery becomes possible. Be proactive in radiating compassion and care. Bring to mind an image of someone you know who is grieving. Close your eyes and allow a positive sentence from your heart to arise, such as, "May you be well and free from suffering." This is a gift whether you say this to them or just carry this sentiment within yourself

Be a witness

It is healthy for someone to cry and let tears flow, whether their loss seems significant to you or not. Do not belittle their experience or trump their story with one of your own. You may want to comfort the other person when they cry, but give them space and do not smother them. Crying is a release. Gently reassure them it is okay to weep or sob, that they do not need to apologize for being a human with feelings. Remain attentive; don't rush or interrupt them. Crying is an act of vulnerability and immense trust.

Be a witness to the other person's grief, without trying to explain it away. If strong emotions surface for the person who is grieving, then sitting in silence with them can be enough. It can be difficult to keep quiet when you know the person you care about is experiencing emotional distress, but you do not have to fill the silence and think of "things to say". Just let the silence be what it is. You are showing love and support by being present.

Suggest a change of scene

Over a hundred years ago, psychologist William James described human thinking as like a pair of scissors: one blade as the internal thought process, the other blade as the physical environment within which thinking takes place. When you change your environment, you change what and how you think. If someone you know is affected by a specific loss, could you offer to go for a walk with them in the countryside or by a river? Fresh air, movement and open views of nature have a catalytic effect on thoughts, mood and energy levels.

Last word

Hopefully, you have found comfort, strength and support within the pages of this book. It has described what grief and loss are, how people grieve and has offered ways to cope with different types of loss. Some ways will work for you and others may not. Know that you are not alone and that you can and will live through grief.

Loss changes you, so remember: there is not something wrong with you, but something significant has happened to you. In time, you can learn and grow through your experience. Although grief takes much, it also gives. You may come to understand yourself and others more, bringing a new appreciation for life and gratitude for what remains.

Wishing you the best for your onward journey.

Resources

Below are the contact details of carefully chosen organizations relating to different types of loss. Feel free to make contact with them for support.

UK-based support:

At A Loss: Offers resources and signposting for bereavement support.
Web: www.ataloss.org
Webchat: GriefChat available through the website

Blue Cross: An animal charity offering specific support on pet loss.
Phone: 0300 790 9903
Web: www.bluecross.org.uk
Instagram: @the_blue_cross

CALM: The Campaign Against Living Miserably, offers help for men on a number of issues.
Helpline (open 5pm–Midnight GMT): 0800 58 58 58
Web: www.thecalmzone.net
Webchat: Live Chat available via website
Instagram: @thecalmzone

Child Bereavement UK: Supporting children and families when a child of any age grieves or dies.
Helpline: 0800 02 888 40
Web: www.childbereavementuk.org
Webchat: Live Chat available via website
Instagram: @childbereavementuk

Cruse Bereavement Care: Supporting people through bereavement.
Helpline: 0808 808 1677
Web: www.cruse.org.uk
Webchat: CruseChat available via website
Instagram: @crusesupport

Dying Matters: A campaign run by Hospice UK to encourage openness about bereavement and dying.
Web: www.hospiceuk.org/our-campaigns/dying-matters

Fertility Network UK: Support, advice and information for anyone affected by fertility issues.
Helpline: 0121 323 5025
Web: www.fertilitynetworkuk.org
Instagram: @fertilitynetworkuk

Good Grief Project: Helping people express bereavement in active and creative ways.
Phone: 07808 472885
Web: www.thegoodgriefproject.co.uk
Instagram: @thegoodgriefproject

Good Grief Trust: Signposting people to support and advice on a wide range of bereavement issues.
Web: www.thegoodgrieftrust.org
Instagram: @thegoodgrieftrust

Hospice UK: Helping people affected by death and dying.
Phone: 020 7520 8200
Web: www.hospiceuk.org
Instagram: @hospice_uk

Loss Foundation: Bereavement support specific to cancer or Covid-19.
Phone: 0300 200 4112
Web: www.thelossfoundation.org
Instagram: @thelossfoundation

Marie Curie: Providing frontline nursing and hospice care, plus support on all aspects of dying, death and bereavement.
Helpline: 0800 090 2309
Web: www.mariecurie.org.uk
Webchat: Online chat via website
Instagram: @mariecurieuk

Miscarriage Association: Offering support and information to those affected by miscarriage, ectopic pregnancy or molar pregnancy.
Helpline: 01924 200799
Web: www.miscarriageassociation.org.uk
Webchat: Online chat via website
Instagram: @miscarriageassociation

National Health Service (NHS): For information and support on a wide range of loss issues.
Web: www.nhs.uk
Instagram: @nhs

Papyrus UK: Offering help and support to prevent suicide.
Helpline: 0800 068 41 41
Text: 07860 039 967
Web: www.papyrus-uk.org
Instagram: @papyrus_uk

Samaritans: Supporting anyone facing difficulty or struggling to cope.
Helpline: 116 123
Web: www.samaritans.org
App: Samaritans Self-Help
Instagram: @samaritanscharity

Sands UK: Supports those affected by the death of a baby.
Phone: 0808 164 3332
Web: www.sands.org.uk
Instagram: @sandscharity

Saying Goodbye: Supporting those who have suffered the loss of a baby at any stage of pregnancy, at birth or in infancy.
Phone: 0300 323 1350
Web: www.sayinggoodbye.org
Instagram: @sayinggoodbye_charity

Sudden: Support and advice in the first ten weeks of a sudden bereavement.
Helpline: 0800 2600 400
Web: www.sudden.org

THRIVE App: A free app, approved by the National Health Service, to support mental well-being.
Web: www.thrive.uk.com

WAY: Widowed and Young provides help for men and women aged fifty and under when their partner has died.
Web: www.widowedandyoung.org.uk
Instagram: @widowedandyoung

Other sources of support:

Festival: Good Grief Festival: Hosting free events, webinars and interviews to normalize the conversation around grief.
www.goodgrieffest.com/resources-and-support/
Instagram: @goodgrieffestival

Podcast: Griefcast: Award-winning podcast with comedians examining human experiences of grief.
Web: www.cariadlloyd.com/griefcast
Instagram: @thegriefcast

International support:

American Counseling Association (ACA): Offering a wide range of publications and courses related to grief and loss.
Phone: 703 823 9801
Web: www.counseling.org
Instagram: @americancounselingassociation

American Psychological Association (APA) Promoting scientific understanding of human behaviour and mental health.
Phone: 800 374 2721 or 202 336 4242
Web: www.apa.org/topics/families/grief
Instagram: @americanpsychologicalassoc

Association for Behavioural and Cognitive Therapies (ABCT): Offering access to trained therapists and research publications.
Phone: 212 647 1890
Web: www.abct.org
Instagram: @abct_insta

Association for Pet Loss and Bereavement (APLB):
Supporting those grieving the loss of a pet.
Web: www.aplb.org
Instagram: @aplb4u

Good Grief (US-based): A charity supporting
grieving children.
Phone: 908 522 1999
Web: www.good-grief.org
Instagram: @goodgriefnj

Grief Haven: A charity providing
grief support and education.
Phone: 310 459 1789
Web: www.griefhaven.org

Healthline: A free web-based resource on wide
range of grief and health-related topics.
Web: www.healthline.com/health/
the-other-side-of-grief-series#1
Web: www.healthline.com/health/mental-
health/suicide-resource-guide
Instagram: @healthline

Mental Health America: (US-based)
Promoting mental health and addressing
the needs of those with mental illness.
Phone: 703 684 7722
Web: www.mhanational.org/bereavement-and-grief
Instagram: @mentalhealthamerica

Samaritans: (US-based)
Supporting anyone facing difficulty or struggling to cope.
Phone: 800 273 TALK
Web: www.samaritansusa.org
Instagram: @samaritanscharity

About the Authors

Christopher Spriggs runs Heads Up Now Ltd., a trauma-informed coaching and consultancy company working with schools across the UK to help people flourish. His first book, *The Reason I Run: How Two Men Transformed Tragedy into the Greatest Race of Their Lives*, told the true story of pushing his terminally ill uncle around a marathon in an NHS wheelchair.

Jess Smallwood is a volunteer for The Mariposa Trust, an international charity primarily supporting those who have experienced the loss of a baby in pregnancy, at birth or in infancy. She has written for a number of publications, organized fundraising events and worked as a learning mentor, supporting young people with special educational needs.

Have you enjoyed this book?
If so, why not write a review on your favourite website?

If you're interested in finding out more about our
books, find us on Facebook at **Summersdale Publishers**,
on Twitter at **@Summersdale** and on Instagram at
@summersdalebooks and get in touch.

Thanks very much for buying this Summersdale book.

www.summersdale.com